Akilia

Restoration
Is
Prohibited
Without
Obedience
Journal

Who does God Say I am?

Date:

Verse of the Day :

Who does God Say I am?

Date:

Verse of the Day :

Who does God Say I am?

Date:

Verse of the Day :

Who does God Say I am?

Date:

Verse of the
Day :

Who does God Say I am?

Date:

Verse of the Day :

Who does God Say I am?

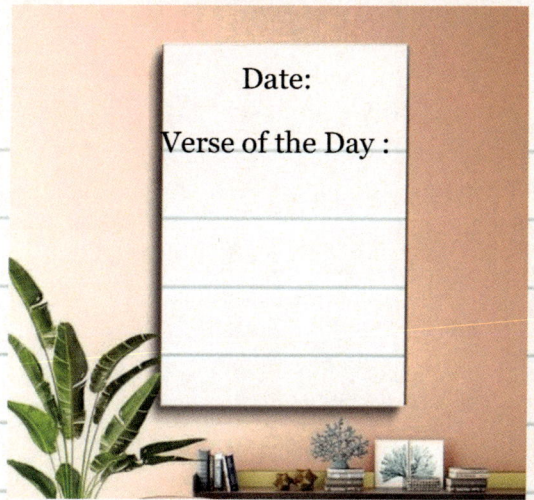

Date:

Verse of the Day :

Who does God Say I am?

Date:

Verse of the Day :

Who does God Say I am?

Date:

Verse of the Day :

Who does God Say I am?

Date:

Verse of the Day :

Who does God Say I am?

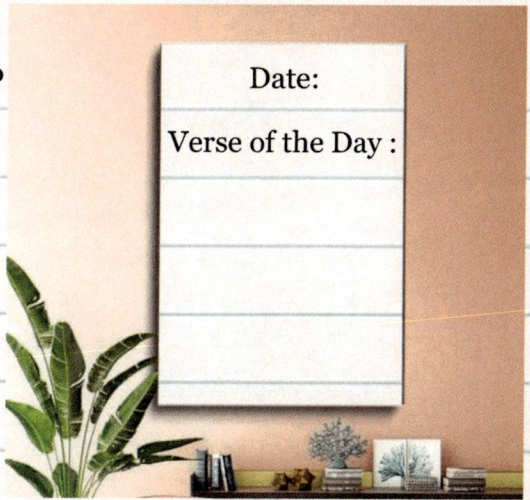

Date:

Verse of the Day :

Who does God Say I

Date:

Verse of the
Day :

Who does God Say I am?

Date:

Verse of the Day :

Who does God Say I am?

Date:

Verse of the Day :

Who does God Say I am?

Date:

Verse of the Day :

Who does God Say I am?

Date:

Verse of the Day :

Who does God Say I am?

Date:

Verse of the Day :

Who does God Say I am?

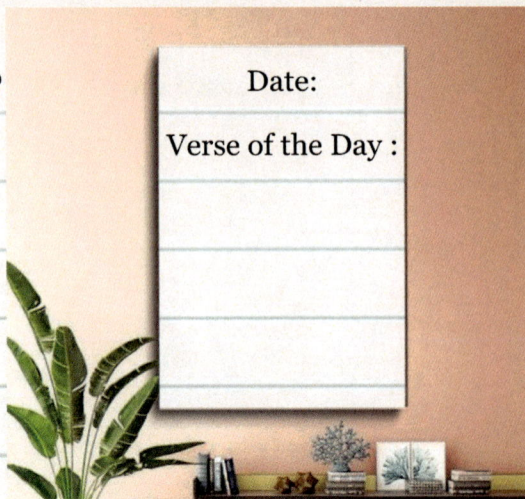

Date:

Verse of the Day :

Who does God Say I am?

Verse of the Day :

Who does God Say I am?

Date:

Verse of the Day :

Who does God Say I am?

Who does God Say I am?

Date:

Verse of the Day :

Who does God Say I am?

Date:

Verse of the Day :

Who does God Say I am?

Date:

Verse of the Day :

Who does God Say I am?

Date:

Verse of the Day :

Who does God Say I

Date:

Verse of the Day :

Who does God Say I am?

Date:

Verse of the Day :

Who does God Say I am?

Date:

Verse of the Day :

Who does God Say I am?

Date:

Verse of the Day :

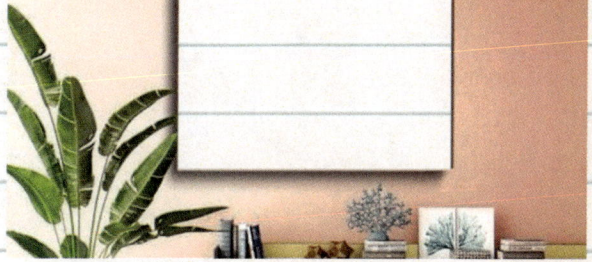

Who does God Say I am?

Date:

Verse of the Day :

Who does God Say I am?

Date:

Verse of the Day :

Who does God Say I am?

Date:

Verse of the Day :

Who does God Say I am?

Date:

Verse of the Day :

Who does God Say I am?

Date:

Verse of the Day :

Who does God Say I am?

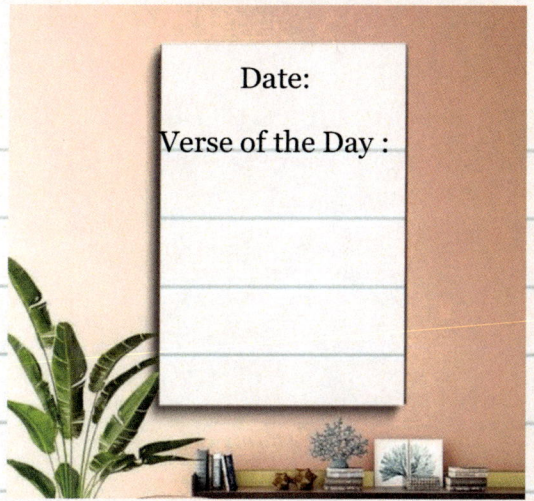

Date:

Verse of the Day :

Who does God Say I am?

Date:

Verse of the Day :

Who does God Say I am?

Date:

Verse of the Day :

Who does God Say I am?

Date:

Verse of the Day :

Who does God Say I am?

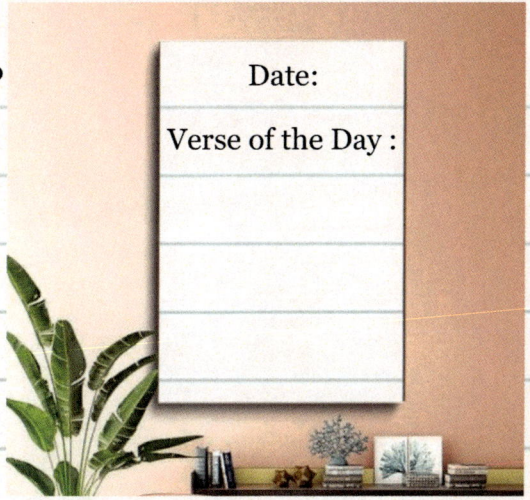

Date:

Verse of the Day :

Who does God Say I

Date:

Verse of the
Day :

Who does God Say I am?

Date:

Verse of the Day :

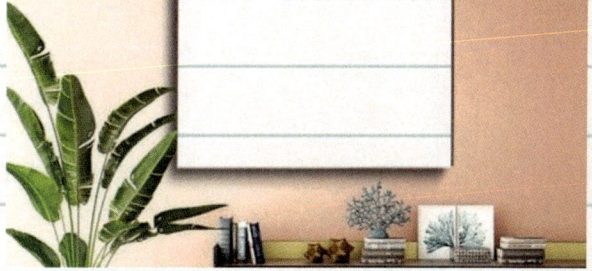

Who does God Say I am?

Date:

Verse of the Day :

Who does God Say I am?

Date:

Verse of the Day :

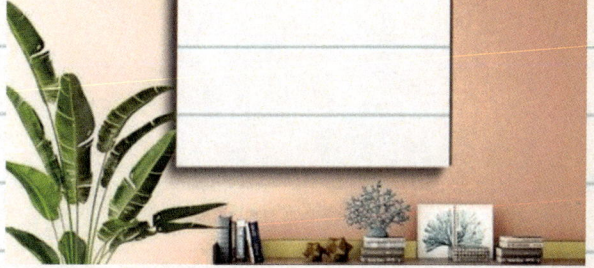

Who does God Say I am?

Date:

Verse of the Day :

Who does God Say I am?

Date:

Verse of the Day :

Who does God Say I am?

Date:

Verse of the Day :

Who does God Say I am?

Date:

Verse of the
Day :

Who does God Say I am?

Date:

Verse of the Day :

Who does God Say I am?

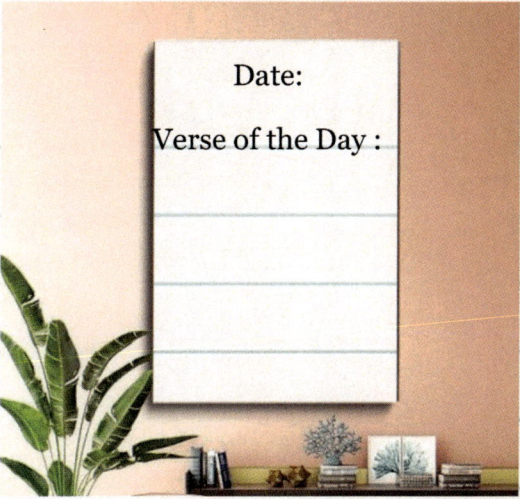

Who does God Say I am?

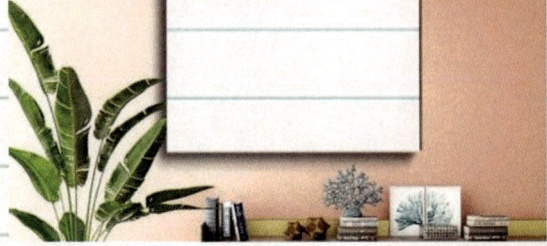

Date:

Verse of the Day :

Who does God Say I am?

Verse of the Day :

Who does God Say I am?

Date:

Verse of the Day :

Who does God Say I am?

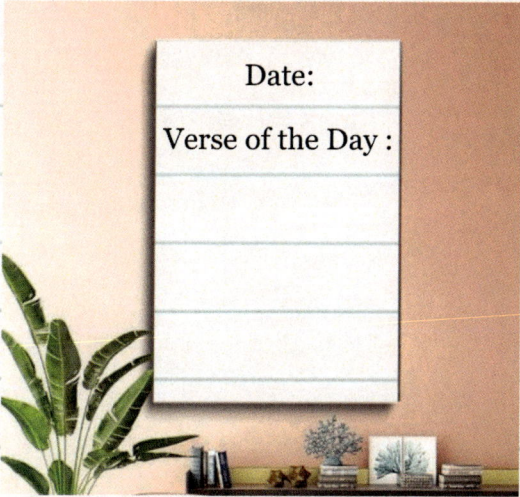

Date:

Verse of the Day :

Who does God Say I

Date:

Verse of the
Day :

Who does God Say I am?

Date:

Verse of the Day :

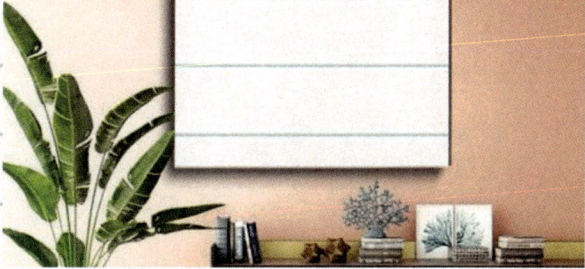

Who does God Say I am?

Date:

Verse of the Day :

Who does God Say I am?

Who does God Say I am?

Date:

Verse of the Day :

Who does God Say I am?

Date:

Verse of the Day :

Who does God Say I am?

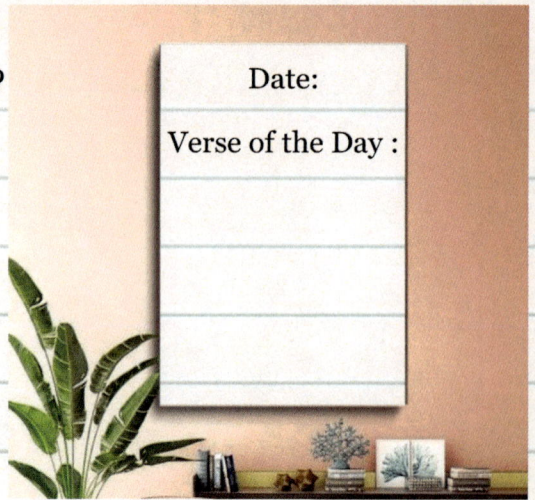

Date:

Verse of the Day :

Who does God Say I am?

Date:

Verse of the Day :

Who does God Say I am?

Date:

Verse of the Day :

Who does God Say I am?

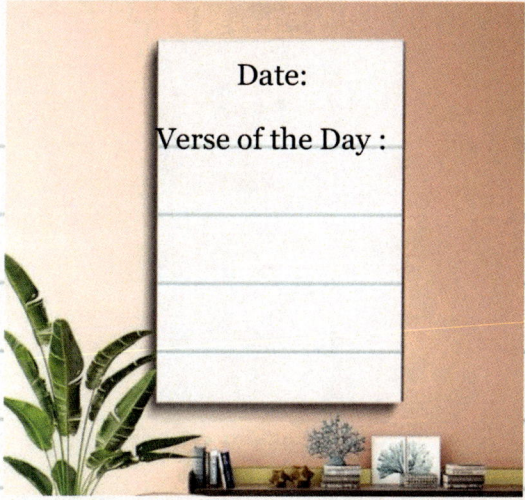

Date:

Verse of the Day :

Who does God Say I am?

Date:

Verse of the Day :

Who does God Say I am?

Date:

Verse of the Day :

Who does God Say I am?

Date:

Verse of the Day :

Who does God Say I am?

Date:

Verse of the Day :

Who does God Say I

Date:

Verse of the
Day :

Who does God Say I am?

Date:

Verse of the Day :

Who does God Say I am?

Date:

Verse of the Day :

Who does God Say I am?

Date:

Verse of the Day :

Who does God Say I am?

Date:

Verse of the Day :

Who does God Say I am?

Date:

Verse of the Day :

Who does God Say I am?

Date:

Verse of the Day :

Who does God Say I am?

Date:

Verse of the
Day :

Who does God Say I am?

Date:

Verse of the Day :

Who does God Say I am?

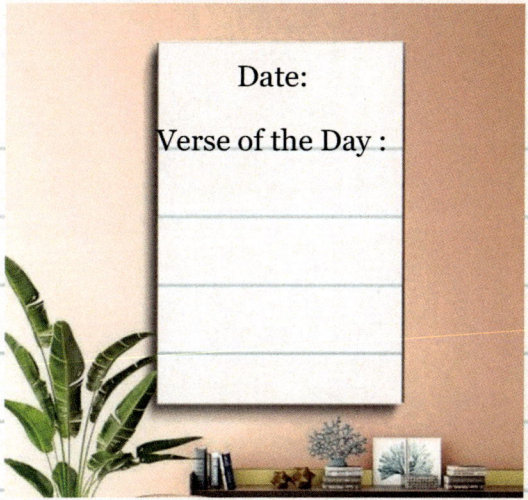

Who does God Say I am?

Date:

Verse of the Day :

Who does God Say I am?

Date:

Verse of the Day :

Who does God Say I am?

Date:

Verse of the Day :

Who does God Say I am?

Date:

Verse of the Day :

Who does God Say I

Date:

Verse of the
Day :

Who does God Say I am?

Date:

Verse of the Day :

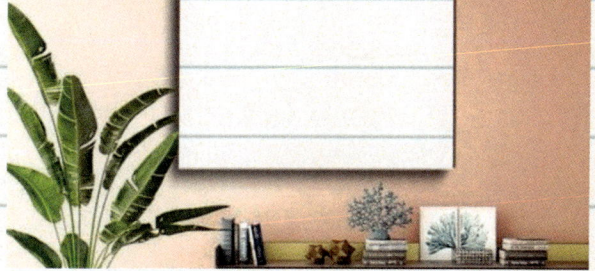

Who does God Say I am?

Date:

Verse of the Day :

Who does God Say I am?

Date:

Verse of the Day :

Who does God Say I am?

Date:

Verse of the Day :

Who does God Say I am?

Date:

Verse of the Day :

Who does God Say I am?

Date:

Verse of the Day :

Who does God Say I am?

Date:

Verse of the
Day :

Who does God Say I am?

Date:

Verse of the Day :

Who does God Say I am?

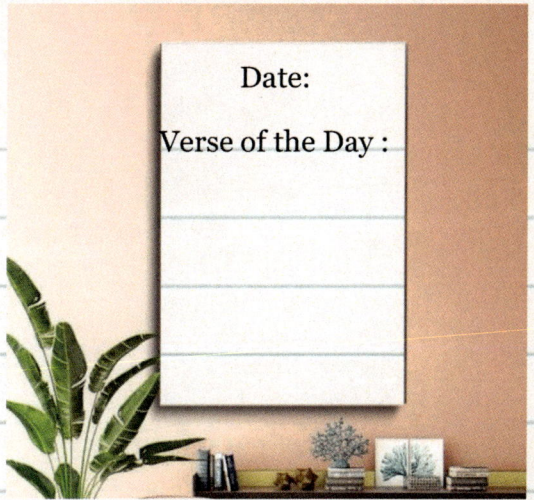

Date:

Verse of the Day :

Who does God Say I am?

Date:

Verse of the Day :

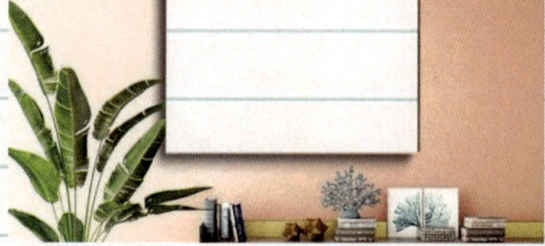

Who does God Say I am?

Date:

Verse of the Day :

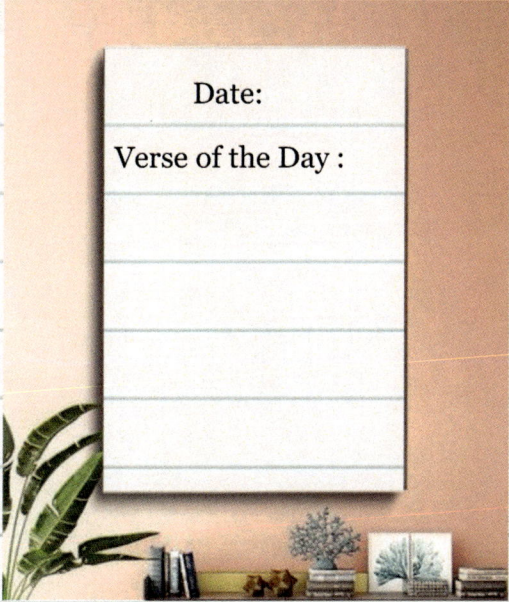

Who does God Say I am?

Date:

Verse of the Day :

Who does God Say I am?

Date:

Verse of the Day :

Who does God Say I

Date:

Verse of the
Day :

Who does God Say I am?

Date:

Verse of the Day :

Who does God Say I am?

Date:

Verse of the Day :

Restoration is prohibited without Obedience

Yet, you utter out of thine lips
"Why, Oh Lord Why?"

Written by, Akilia Fortier

Copyright 2021

Made in the USA
Coppell, TX
29 July 2021